HASSLING
FOR FUN AND PROFIT

How can you save time on the job?
> *Read mail and answer phone calls while in conversation with an employee.*

Why should you call meetings?
> *So you can cancel them at the last minute.*

What is the purpose of employee vacations?
> *Gives you a chance to rifle through their desks and see what they're really up to.*

What is the best way to make a point?
> *At the top of your lungs.*

What is the best way ~~to~~ ...age?

MANAGEMENT BY HASSLING

An Irreverent Guide to the Art of Management

Jim Kuhn

Illustrations by Don Margolis

FAWCETT CREST • NEW YORK

A Fawcett Crest Book
Published by Ballantine Books
Copyright © 1988 by Jim Kuhn

All rights reserved under International and Pan-American Copyright Conventions. Published in the United States by Ballantine Books, a division of Random House, Inc., New York, and simultaneously in Canada by Random House of Canada Limited, Toronto. This book was previously self-published in 1988.

Library of Congress Catalog Card Number: 92-90146

ISBN 0-449-22106-7

Manufactured in the United States of America

First Edition: August 1992

To Anne,
for her support and help
in search of the ultimate hassle.

INTRODUCTION

HASSLING
THE CONTROVERSIAL AND LONG-OVERLOOKED MANAGEMENT ART

There have been many management ideas in the past and volumes of literature on modern management methods. A recent one is Management by Objectives. However, one key area of management theory remains unnoticed, untouched, and until now, unexplored. You won't find it in the business schools, you won't find it in the textbooks, and yet it has been used successfully for years.

It is the long-overlooked and under-communicated art of hassling.

While hassling is as old as management itself, there is apparently no literature dealing with its methodology and its unique place in the tool kits of modern-day managers.

So we have decided to break new ground and bring to our people a better grasp of this elusive subject. The purpose of this book is to communicate clearly the art of the successful hassle.

We call it—MANAGEMENT BY HASSLING—

M. B. H.

BACKGROUND

It is the author's goal to help supervisors develop this interesting and useful skill. We will do this with actual illustrations of successful hassles, rather than extensive analytical verbiage. This way our readers will be able to learn by example. Each of these brief illustrations of hassling situations has actually proved successful in our own company.

This is interesting, since we feared our initial research would have to cover many companies. We were wrong. Fortunately, we found we already possessed considerable expertise right in our own organization, and all that was needed was to bring it to the surface.

Several things became evident during our research. We found that while most people hassle, some don't know how to hassle, and others don't want to. Many will want to carry this book in a brown paper bag because hassling is controversial.

SOME FACTS ABOUT HASSLING

Hassling is a skill that can be developed to very sophisticated levels. It can become so second nature that once it is mastered, people hardly know they're doing it. Like the piano player who can sing and play at the same time, a master hassler is able to undertake all his normal duties while hassling, without interruption.

Hassling isn't only things we say. It can be words we don't say or things we don't do, or gestures or frowns. In short, it can be done in so many ways that the potential is astounding.

Most hassling is a series of little things. But the beauty of it is that even without a plan, enough small hassles accumulate so well that we can convince an employee that we don't care for him or her at all, even when we really do.

One of the greatest things supporters of hassling claim is that it takes very little effort to achieve fantastic and devastating results. They report that it is far easier both to install and follow up a hassling program than it is with any other management system. They indicate that it is a positively amazing motivational tool. So powerful is this tool that a few well-placed hassles can even get an employee to resign.

SUCCESSFUL HASSLING

So much for background and facts. As we said earlier, the best way to learn about hassling is to study actual hassles. On the following pages, we have listed forty-nine of the most successful hassles found to date. We recognize that since our initial research only covered a few months, there must be more out there. We think the scope of the successful hassle is infinite.

We hope that you, our reader, if you are stimulated by this new management art, will forward other successful hassles to us, both to further our knowledge and understanding of hassling and for possible future printings of this original research publication.

You will notice that we have numbered each hassle, so that if an employee wishes to call your attention to particularly successful ones, he or she need only identify it by number, saving considerable time and energy.

The writings and drawings may make it appear that these hassles are best suited to office situations. This is not the case. With a little variation, almost every hassle has been proved successful in any kind of workplace and with every kind of employee. The nonspecific background for presenting them was chosen to show that they can work anywhere and in any organization.

We now present the forty-nine most successful hassles we have available at this time.

MANAGEMENT BY HASSLING

1

Look at your watch while saying, "Sure, I've always got time for you."

2

Don't tell employees you're upset with them, so you can avoid hurting their feelings. This also permits them to imagine that whatever is bothering you is really worse than it is.

3

Don't praise people too much; they may get cocky and slack off.

4

When people really screw up, be sure to tell
not only them but everyone within earshot.
This shows that you are both sharp and
willing to face tough problems.

5

When people goof, don't bother to praise them for really trying, despite the failure, because results are all that matter.

Don't show your real emotions to your people. By being truly unemotional, you can get them so confused about what you really believe or are feeling that they will hold you in awe.

7

Maintain your authority by canceling
meetings because higher-ups called you.
This can be even better if you do it at the
last minute or don't bother to let the people
know at all.

8

Don't explain any confidential things to your employees, because they can't understand, can't be trusted, or don't care.

Never walk out of your office to see the people you want. After all, you have an open-door policy, so anyone who wants you can come to you.

10

Always remind minorities and women that you don't have any prejudices.

11

Always ask your secretary to get coffee or lunch, even though you need the exercise and once in a while could reciprocate and get hers.

12

Chew people out for not having something done, and give them a week to do it. When you follow up and notice it has been done, don't mention it. Find something else. This way they'll always be on their toes.

13

Don't take the time to bounce your ideas off of people working on similar things in other departments—they may steal them.

14

Never tell why something is being done,
because you're really much too busy.

15

Never socialize with people of lower job levels than you, particularly your own subordinates; or at least keep them at a proper distance, as you might weaken your authority.

16

Don't ask your employees what they want for the future; they'll probably just ask for a raise. Besides, the corporation is all that matters.

17

Always keep people waiting for performance reviews or other important meetings. It helps enhance your status and serves to remind employees that you are very busy.

18

When people goof, after apologies have
been made, quietly keep reminding them of
their error so that they won't do it again.

19

Don't admit your mistakes to your subordinates; they may lose respect for you or not appreciate your authority.

20

When you hear harsh criticism about people, don't bother to get their side of the story. That takes a lot of time and may be embarrassing; and, besides, your good judgment can determine what's right.

21

Don't tell people who are not likely to be promoted where they really stand. You might demotivate them or even lose them.

22

Preserve professional dignity by never talking about anything other than business.

23

Don't hurt employees' feelings by telling them that they are near the top of their pay range or explaining why their raise was a small one. They should be able to figure these things out for themselves.

24

Give all your employees the same or similar performance ratings to prevent conflicts from arising if they should discover any differences.

25

When employees ask to learn things outside of the present job, don't answer them. After all, they don't need to know that stuff; they have enough work of their own.

26

Don't admit weakness by asking your people to help with special problems.

27

Don't let a valuable employee leave your department for another one unless it's a major promotion. It costs too much time and money to train a replacement.

Don't ask too many questions of your
people. After all, a good supervisor knows
more than his people do.

29

Never take your people to lunch.

30

Don't say "Hi" when you pass someone in the hall. You're too busy rushing to a meeting.

31

Never fire anyone; it isn't nice. Besides, this way everyone can be so unsure about what it takes to get fired that they will all fear for their jobs.

32

Don't allow people to take vacation in one lump of time when they want it; it messes up the work flow too much.

33

Always have minority employees handle matters related to minority relations—they're truly experts.

34

Never meddle in your people's personal lives by asking how their families are or what hobbies or interests they have. These things are not professional.

35

Knock other departments or locations in order to build the pride of your own people.

36

Never ask yourself if you could be the reason something went wrong or how you might have helped avoid it. After all, the probability of your being wrong is highly unlikely, and your people might think less of you.

37

If you have a problem working with employees not directly under your supervision, don't try to work out a solution with them—go to the employees' supervisors and lodge your complaint. Better yet, publicize the situation and trust the grapevine to relay your message back.

38

Assign a project, stressing how valuable it is and how important deadlines are. When the employee crawls in after putting in sixteen-hour days and weekends, toss it aside and promise to read the results soon. Be sure to never mention the report again.

39

When changing a policy or procedure, don't bother to explain why. It takes too much time, and people need to respect authority anyway.

40

Save time by reading your mail while an employee talks to you.

41

Tell people to take off the days they've been missing, and then be sure to inspect everything they've been doing while they're gone. To increase the effectiveness, chew them out when they return for things they might have missed.

42

If you are having a meeting with one of your people and someone of higher authority walks in unexpectedly, be sure to break up the meeting.

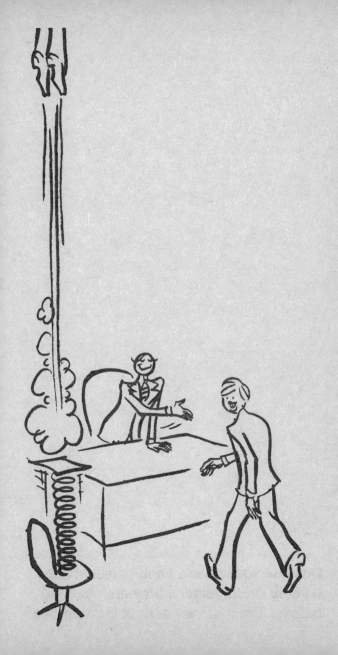

43

Don't let your people keep personal effects on their desks, even if they are neat and orderly. These things are not businesslike.

44

Be sure that employees' paychecks are late, and double the effect by not returning their calls when they try to find out what happened.

45

Tell people you care about their families but continue to start meetings on Sunday.

46

Don't worry about your people's performance reviews. After all, they know where they stand, and if they don't they can ask.

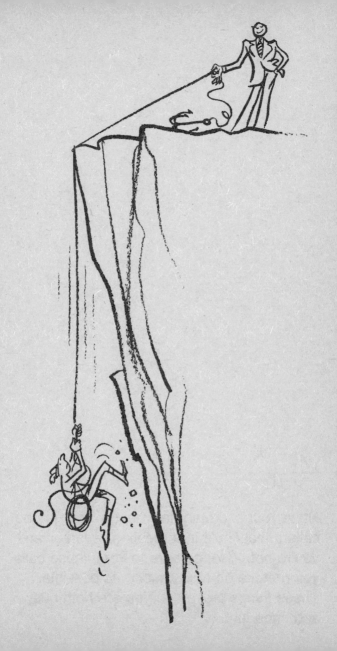

47

Have your secretary tell most of your phone callers that "he's in a meeting" even when you're not. Also, be sure to keep those calls you do take on hold as long as possible. These things prove that you are both busy and important.

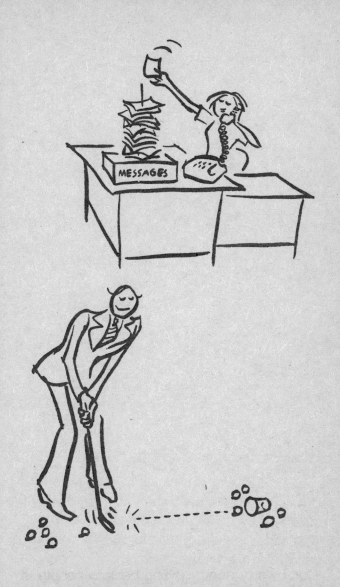

48

Don't worry about getting back to people. If it's really important, they'll get back to you.

49

Tell employees they look tired and they've been working too hard. Then return later with a new assignment. Increase the effect by asking a week later why they aren't finished.

THANKS

Special thanks to the people whose talents and hard work produced this book—including:

Elaine Classen, Marge Cooke, Denis Detzel, Helen Farrell, Ron Gier, Al Golin, Stan Greenberg, Kevin Heniff, John Horwitz, Noel Kaplan, Sid Kaplan, Don Lorr, Lucy Ostrom, Sharmayne Prats, Carolyn Reid, Ed Rensi, Celeste Roberts, Don Schuler, Mike Sembrat, Stan Stein, Pam Thompson, Doug Timberlake, Frank Tuma, Kathleen Wall, and Candy Wilson.

And to Anne, Beth, and Julie Kuhn for believing in me.

MOST OF ALL TO THE HUMAN SPIRIT FOR PROVIDING LIMITLESS EXCITEMENT, HUMOR, UNPREDICTABILITY, AND, OF COURSE, HASSLES.

About the Author

Jim Kuhn recently retired from McDonald's Corporation after twenty-nine years. He was McDonald's first vice-president of personnel, and since 1976, vice-president—Individuality. MANAGEMENT BY HASSLING was originally written as an internal training tool for the company. Kuhn has an A.B. in Psychology from Indiana University and an M.S. in Industrial Psychology from Purdue. He loves to spend time with his family, swim, canoe, bicycle, and laugh.